The author – Vince Morris, 5th Dan

Zanshin

Meditation and the Mind in Modern Martial Arts

by
Vince Morris

SAMUEL WEISER, INC.

York Beach, Maine

First American edition published in 1992 by
Samuel Weiser, Inc.
Box 612
York Beach, ME 03910

01 00 99 98 97 96 95
10 9 8 7 6 5 4 3 2

Library of Congress Cataloging-in-Publication Data
Morris, P. M. V. (P. M. Vince)
  Zanshin : meditation and the mind in martial arts /
  by Vince Morris
      p. cm.
   Includes bibliographial references.
    1. Martial arts—Psychological aspects. 2. Meditation—
  Zen Buddhism. I. Title.
  GV1101.M666 1992
    796.8—dc20   92-1758
  ISBN 0-87228-756-2   CIP
  BJ

Cover painting copyright © 1992 Rob Schouten.
Used by kind permission of the artist.

Printed in the United States of America

I would like to dedicate this work to Shiro Asano, to whom I owe a deep debt of gratitude for so many things; to my valued friend and colleague Aidan Trimble; and to all of my students who – knowingly or not – have helped me on the way.

Contents

Acknowledgments   ix

Introduction   xi

1 What is meditation and how does it work ?   1

2 Types of meditation   11

3 The historical evidence   23

4 The contemporary evidence   39

5 How to meditate   43

6 'If'   53

7 Mental rehearsal and visualisation   59

8 How to combine meditation with physical
   practice   63

9 The technique   71

10 The first attempt – an analysis of stress   75

11 A final note   81

About the author   87

Notes to the text   91

Recommended books and works consulted   95

Acknowledgments

As usual, I would like to thank Roddy Bloomfield and Dominique Shead at Stanley Paul for their continual support and encouragement, not to mention lunches. My thanks to Neil Sutcliffe for his competition report. I would also like to say 'Thank you' to the Embassy of Japan and to all my friends who have supplied most of the photographs for this work.

Introduction

You may find this book exasperating. You may find that it doesn't necessarily follow every train of thought to a conclusion. Then again you may find that it suddenly returns to a topic touched upon earlier. Good!

All I want is to perhaps provide a starting-point for your own thinking. There is so much that I could write, so many avenues to explore, but eventually it would all be for nothing if you found it satisfying and complete in itself.

The power of the human mind is vast and mostly untapped. We are prepared to spend years training our bodies to cope with the demands of both life and our choice of martial art, but we mostly neither know nor appear to care about the one thing which, in the end, will either enhance or undermine our physical effectiveness.

> Few people realise that the journey from schoolboy medalist to Olympic Champion is very much a mental one.
>
> *(Lynn Davies, Olympic Gold Medalist)*

Anyone who has practised a martial art in some depth over a reasonable period of time will, if asked, acknowledge that there is a significant difference between the 'feel' of this practice and that of other – on the surface equally competitive and demanding – sports.

Even other combat sports such as Boxing, Fencing, Wrestling, and other physical contact games like Football, Rugby, Lacrosse, etc., which often produce physical confrontations, do not produce the tangible intensity of atmosphere generated when two martial experts are face to face, when time seems to slow, and nothing exists in the whole universe, except that infinitesimal millisecond when a strike is initiated, anticipated and countered with deadly force and total commitment!

This work aims to examine that difference; to illuminate not just the inner workings of the minds of historical and contemporary martial experts, but to indicate why the differences exist, and to lay down a guide which will enable anyone with sufficient application to learn and follow the techniques which make the martial arts stand apart.

To look only at this aspect, however important, would be to do a grave disservice. There is also another great difference between a martial art and a sport that must be examined. For it is claimed that anyone studying and practising a martial art diligently will develop an indomitable spirit, tremendous self-reliance, and the ability to perform 'Right Action' in difficult circumstances. The questions are, then: 'Is this true?' and 'How?'

Of course, in these days of 'instant Black-Belts', there will be some who will say that practice in technique alone will bring this about: all one needs is mastery of the kicks, throws, strikes and blocks, then all else will follow through diligent repetition of the *Waza*, the mechanics of the movements. Believe me, *this is not true!*

There is a special quality which comes from a harmonisation of physical and cerebral function; a certain strength which comes from within, not manifested in outward 'Macho' display, and which will serve as a constant bedrock from which to comprehend and face life's many vicissitudes with calm equanimity. This can *never* be solely the product of mechanical repetition!

A serious martial artist will understand that the journey along the path of his or her art is not simply directed towards mastery of the art itself, but towards an even more remote and elusive goal – that of realising potential; of fulfilling the promise inherent in each newborn infant, a continual striving towards an ever unattainable comprehension and adulthood which comes from the constant facing of truths, be they physical or emotional.

A martial art is never just for the *Dojo*, something like a game of Badminton, which can be the total focus of attention and effort for a short period, but which can be forgotten once off the court. No: life for the martial artist is a continual series of encounters from which he or she sometimes emerges victorious, sometimes defeated, but – more often than not – comes to accept a bruising stalemate. The point is, however, that they are always *useful* encounters. In my eyes, it is really wrong, anyway, to think of oneself learning or practising the martial arts. Being a martial artist is not what you do but what you are.

Gichin Funakoshi, the 'Father' of Karate, who was responsible for the introduction of this fighting art onto the Japanese mainland soon found that his envelopment in and exposure to the existing martial arts and their all-pervading ethic gave him cogent reasons for changing the characters which construed 'China (Chinese) Hand' into the homophones meaning 'Empty Hand' and adding the suffix '-do'.

Thus 'Tang-te' (Kara-te) became 'Karate-do', placing the art firmly in the traditional ethos of '-Ways' which for hundreds of years had laid emphasis upon the character-building foundation of Buddhist (and in particular *Zen* Buddhist) philosophy and practice.

Of course there were no doubt political encouragements to this change, given the Japanese dislike of any 'foreign' device or art, but any reasonable study of Funakoshi's life story and writings must admit that his overriding concern was to emphasise the character-developing features of the art, and also the philosophical concepts, standing the art upon a base of strength, integrity and peacefulness.

He would actually stress that the true karate student should be like an empty valley, which because of its emptiness can carry a resounding voice; the student should rid himself of all self-centredness and greed, being empty within, upright without. This, he said, was the true meaning of 'empty' in karate.

These elements were not – as has been suggested – brought about only following his exposure to the mainland martial ways, but were features of the Okinawan fighting arts as traditionally taught by such masters as Itosu and Higaonna.[1]

The nature of a true martial art, being in essence to transcend the 'self', uses the warp and weft of daily life with all its successes and failures to continually refine and develop the spiritual/psychological centre of the practitioner.

Thus whilst we talk of 'Triumph and Disaster' . . . those two impostors which may be understandable and make sense on the mundane, everyday level, the reality is that, as the nineteenth-century poet and philosopher Nietzsche put it: 'That which does not destroy us makes us stronger.' So, what might on the face of it may seem setbacks, can by no stretch of logic or semantics be deemed failure, or 'Disaster'.

One of the great secrets of the martial arts, as Kodo Sawaki used to say, is that you can neither win nor be beaten, for there is no victory and no defeat.[2] So the reason for my attempt at writing this book is really twofold. On the one hand as a Karate *sensei* I believe strongly that the sheer efficiency of the technical side of the martial art can be much improved by utilising the powers of the mind to the full. I rely here not just on evidence from within the martial arts sphere, but also on direct and anecdotal evidence from a variety of other disparate athletic and sporting disciplines.

On the other hand I also firmly believe that as human beings we are born into this world with vast potential, and that life is a growing process, not only towards physical maturity, but towards mental, psychological and spiritual adulthood.

We are happy to accept medical help towards ensuring our physical growth, and social help towards aiding our education in order to help us to achieve physical security and prosperity. All too often, however, we balk at the realisation that just as we (as Martial Artists/Athletes) continue to train and care for our physical shells throughout our lives, so we must continue to give time and effort to continuing our internal training and education over the same time scale. 'Mens sana in corpore sano' was the Classical ideal, but a healthy mind in a healthy body cannot possibly be achieved if only one part of the equation receives attention whilst the other is neglected.

I would like to draw a distinction, however, between 'Education', in the narrow sense of learning facts, figures and technical skills, and the type of inner training that I am advocating. The former will equip you to lead a life with certain skills and accomplishments, and will provide knowledge of the external world for you to make use of in whatever way you wish. The type I will be discussing in this work is of a different nature.

It is based on a 'self-knowledge', an informed and (I hesitate to use the word) 'enlightened' understanding of yourself and the world, and of your place in it and as a part of it. This bedrock of comprehension will provide the base for the former type to take root in and flourish.

I do not – by the way – claim that the concepts are in any way new. On the contrary, many date back thousands of years. The trouble is that many of the ideas are often inaccessibly couched in dogma and quite unwarranted mysticism. This is more than unfortunate; it is a tragedy!

After more than thirty years' exposure to these concepts, and of my own experience in trying to put them into some sort of order and relevance to today's world, I have come to some conclusions which I pass on here for you to do with as you wish. I think no advice could be better than Budda's: 'Test it and see if it works. If it does, then use it. If it doesn't, then throw it away!'

In my search for answers I have spent much time in contemplation and meditation, in a variety of disciplines, both religious and secular, Eastern and Western, as well as having spent more than 30 years in serious study and practice of the martial arts. I don't claim to have arrived at any absolute conclusions (except to affirm that there are indeed many different paths leading to the top of a mountain).

None the less, I have lived a very full and varied life, often under great stress for one reason or another, and I have come to formulate a synthesis of the diverse concepts, which does seem to work, and which has (for me, being a very pragmatic – and sceptical – person) the advantage of being testable, of having a real physical result, and which makes *sense*!

1 What is meditation and how does it work?

It is understood that what marks a Martial Art as different from a Martial system of techniques is that there are concomitants, other things going along with the simply technical concerns of defeating an opponent. These 'other things' are often described as 'Enlightenment', 'Satori', 'Zanshin' and such-like, together with certain characteristics and accomplishments like: integrity, compassion, courage, dignity, a cool head, good manners and so on. We all know this, don't we?

The fact is, however, that in the vast majority of Martial Arts Dojos throughout the world by far the greater part of the time spent in practice is spent on learning and mastering technique. Little or no time is given over to the study of – even less the practice of – whatever it is that brings along these accompanying attributes: meditation and methods of enhancing the powers of mental concentration.

When the body is in its normal state, a condition of chemical and hormonal balance, it has tremendous capacity for self-healing. Doctors may splint a broken leg, but it is the body itself that carries out the repair. The immune system fights to repel harmful invasions and to restore the normal healthy condition.

In today's world, however, the stresses of everyday life often have an unsettling and debilitating effect upon the whole body and its nervous system. This impairs the functioning of the immune and regulatory system so that the body is unable to maintain its healthy state, or regain it when under attack by illness or disease.

Using meditation as a tool for deep relaxation and to quieten the mind helps to alleviate the stress and therefore enable the internal chemical and hormonal systems to regain their equilibrium. Then the immune and regulatory systems can carry out their designated functions, creating a balance between the active and the passive, the Yin and Yang.

Medical tests have shown that there are very definite measurable physiological changes in meditating subjects.[3] The brain itself undergoes subtle changes in the type of electrical wave generated. Using an electroencephalograph there is shown to be an increase in the generation of what are termed *Alpha* waves and sometimes *Theta*. These indicate a shift of consciousness into a state of restful awareness, quite different from that of sleep, but which can be very restful, and therapeutic.

The Alpha state is also most conducive to creativity and to the assimilation of new concepts, whilst the Theta level seems to be a stage at which the mind is capable of deep insights and intuition. Significantly, practised meditators can continue to exhibit Alpha and Theta waves after the meditation period has ended.

The body demonstrates the effects of meditation in various ways. The breathing pattern slows, as does the heart rate. There is a marked decrease in the level of oxygen utilisation and carbon dioxide elimination, and an increase in galvanic skin response (electrical resistance).

That the physical effects of meditation linger on after the meditation period itself has ended is demonstrable by the fact that sufferers of hypertension and high blood pressure have – through meditation alone – made such clinically measurable improvements that they have been able to become completely free of drug treatment.

Leaving the questioning/searching type of meditation aside for a moment, the act of sitting in quiet, calm stillness, acts as a wonderfully effective stress-relieving device, making us better able to function in the hurly-burly of modern life.

Of course, we mustn't assume that all stress is bad: this is far from the truth. A certain degree of stress is necessary in most situations in order to provide the stimulus needed to encourage us into action. Sexual stimulation evokes the desired response; the visual stimulation of our favourite food provokes salivation; challenges at work evince creativity and motivation, and so on.

But there comes a point where the degree of stress actually works against encouraging the proper response. Sexual desire is inhibited, appetite decreases, and we would rather take days off sick than face the pressures of work. We can often see (or our friends and family can) the warning signals of too much stress. We become short-tempered and irritable, we develop acid indigestion and headaches and everything seems too much trouble. If ignored, these initial minor symptoms can turn into life-threatening ulcers, strokes and heart attacks.

In fact the statistics of – for example – the American Academy of Physicians show that of all the visits made to general practitioners in the USA at least two-thirds are for stress-related illnesses.

In actuality, of course, it is not the degree of stress at all that matters; it is simply our ability to cope with it, and this ability can be strengthened and enhanced. Stress, effectively managed, is constructive; whilst stress beyond our ability to cope is destructive. The good thing about meditation as a relaxation tool is that it works quite regardless of the sources or type of stress involved.

The cortex of the human brain can, in a shorthand way, be thought of as being in two halves, often called the left and right hemispheres. Now although I recognise that this is simplistic, and does not even consider the role of the hypothalamus or the evolutionary earlier brain-stem, it is widely considered that the activities such as speech, logical thinking, analysis, time and order recognition, and so on, are seated in the left hemisphere, whilst the ability to appreciate music and art, recognise faces, comprehend maps and form a comprehensive overview of any situation, is seated in the right. (In fact, topographic considerations of 'Right' or 'Left' are immaterial to the unquestionable fact that man functions as a split-brain creature, regardless of the precise site of the origins of each ability.) Most untrained people, under scientific measurement, demonstrate a marked preponderance towards left-hemisphere usage.

Analysis of the patterns of brainwaves produced by thousands of subjects including Zen Masters, healers, mediums, Yogis and others who have been able to demonstrate unusual abilities, have shown a marked integration of left and right hemispheres of the brain, synchronising the logical with the intuitive. Meditation, especially of the Soto Zen, non-discriminatory sort, wherein one is aware of all around, but does not concentrate on nor label any specific thing, is a fine tool for bringing about this integration.

Zen *Koan* meditation, a more disciplined analytical, introspective and searching type than the simple stress-relieving practice, strives towards achieving a deeper and a more accurate view of reality, an understanding of 'Who am I?' and 'Where am I going?' And perhaps more basically: 'Who is the "Self" that is doing the looking?' (I always

The stress shows in the faces and body language of Vince and team members in this photo taken before a Championship Final match.

find it amusing when people say: 'I didn't want to do it, but I made myself!' – who is it, I wonder, that is doing the making?) This was the type of meditation which lay at the heart of the Samurai's practice.

Hojo Tokiyori (1227–1263) was Shogun in the Kamakura era, and he was the first of a long line of Shoguns who saw the value of Zen training for the Samurai. He realised that Zen helped the practitioner to transcend what to us in the West underpins our whole outlook on life, that is Reasoning and Logic, and to go beyond purely rational deductive thinking and develop an intuitive perception of any situation.

The Zen-trained swordsman, for example, was so calmly concentrated on his opponent that he did not have to waste precious split-seconds in analysing his every move and devising counterploys. No, *Zanshin* cut through the mainly left-brain reasoning and allowed his body to react on the instant as if by instinct.

The continual Zen emphasis on pressing the mind further and further on into realms beyond the mundane, bringing the meditator time and again to face the realities of his transient existence and into acceptance of his ultimate end, also had the desired effect of removing the fear of dying.

Thus combat efficiency was further enhanced; for if the Samurai was not in the least afraid of his enemy, if he could not be overawed or 'psyched-out' by fearsome appearance and boasting, then his body was free to function at optimum level.

> I discovered that the way of the Samurai is death!
>
> (*Hagakure*, Book 1)

Meditation, being essentially a solitary practice even when carried out in groups, is often portrayed as, or seen as, an end in itself – particularly when a student sets out on a quest for 'Enlightenment', indeed is encouraged to do so by teachers such as myself. The practice of Soto Zen, with its emphasis on just sitting, on the face of it, gives this impression.

If this were so, however, then meditation would be purely a selfish quest. Not so: it should bear fruit in everyday expression, and should transform and permeate every act. One whose actions are based on wisdom and knowledge will be a source of strength in the community.

He or she will be able to give direction and support, and act as a rock in the storm-tossed seas of modern life with its lack of moral and spiritual purpose. Of course, this tends to make the meditator sound like a candidate for sainthood!

Well, the 'Way' does lead upward, but rather as an enhancement of humanity than as a denial of it. The aim is to become a fully developed person, able to achieve an integrated view of both the immediate concerns and the universal picture.

The practice of the martial way, plus the meditation, should lead to a far greater awareness of one's place in the scheme of things, and is conducive to the desire for 'Right' as opposed to 'Wrong' actions, for harmony rather than discord, for truth instead of falsehood.

For most of us, however, this is not an easy task but a struggle, and one in which we many times fail to live up to even our own poor standards. Often it seems that it would be marvellous just to drop everything and vanish into a retreat, like monks or hermits (or even some karate masters) of old. This would be escapism, however, and although perhaps we could attain the sought-after enlightenment in this way, it would not, I think, be true enlightenment.

Frankly, it seems to me that keeping one's mental balance and practising *Satori* is a much simpler task when one is hidden away from the stresses and strains of life, work and family, in the solitude of a monk's cell or a mountain retreat.

The real test is: how is your equilibrium in an emergency, or after a couple of hours in a traffic jam, or during a sickbed vigil over a seriously ill child?[4] These are moments when the calm centre is vital, and the moments least conductive to achieving or maintaining it.

Essentially, you can see that prolonged contemplative meditation really does force one to come face to face with mortality. It also leads to an acceptance of the illusory nature of such things as fame and fortune.

Nothing lasts for ever, and in the end it all comes to the same conclusion. Even this vast, incomprehensible universe will one day pass out of existence, as will everything in it. For us, of course, the end will probably come somewhat sooner, and no-one can know when that moment will arrive.

Therefore the Samurai was encouraged to begin each day by spending some time in the rehearsing of his own demise. Then his martial practice would reinforce the probability that it would be sudden, and could be at any time.

Thus Zen promoted acceptance of the transient nature of humanity and the universe, and used this awareness as a tool for overcoming fear and inhibited, deviant and erroneous responses. Removal of false perceptions then gave room for proper response.

This was the basis of the Samurai's strength. Lip-service to a philosophy would not have been sufficient, not when life or death in combat were the stakes. Zen philosophy must have permeated the very depths of their psyche to have had such an effect.

One of the recurring metaphors in Buddhist literature is that of the mirror – indicating that cognition (proper seeing) not some esoteric trance-like state is an essential requirement for enlightenment. The perfectly polished mirror reflects things perfectly, without distortion, and the perfectly polished mind sees everything without the distortions of prejudice and fear.

We are aware of the world, and we live in it, but we can do so either deceived by its apparent solidity and reality, or in a state of enlightenment; this being an awareness of the reality which lies behind the appearance. As human beings we are totally dependent upon our senses for our appreciation and understanding of the world, and if we are not very careful we can be deluded into thinking that the apparent reality is the only reality.

As an analogy, imagine a radio set, which only has FM and AM wavebands. A listener would be quite unable to receive any broadcasts on Long Wave or Short Wave. Nothing could be heard from any station other than that which was on the FM and AM bands. If this listener were to insist that only these two bands existed, because they were the only ones that he was immediately aware of, you would understandably consider his view to be illogical. We, however, are more than capable of making the same sort of mistake when 'tuned in' only to the most immediate evidences of 'reality'.

The world as we perceive it does not appear in the same way to the multifaceted eyes of the fly, nor to the colour-blind eyes of a dog, and to a fish the world is an entirely different sort of place. But which version of reality is 'True'?

Our ears are deaf to the high frequencies discernible to canines; does that mean that they do not exist? To our senses a wooden table is a very solid thing; under a high-powered microscope a different reality of tremendously fast-moving atoms and electrons hurtling through vast stretches of empty space is revealed. Our sense of sight tells us that stars are tiny bright specks in the sky; knowledge (reason) tells us that this is not so: a straightforward lesson in the value of 'right seeing'.

To a creature of the flat two-dimensional world (with length and breadth but no height) a three-dimensional object would be miraculous and not believed. If you could talk intelligently to a caterpillar, and tell it that it would cease to exist in its present form, but would one day be reborn as a glorious creature with gossamer wings, it would do its best to get you committed to the insect-world equivalent of the madhouse!

'Ah, but we know better!' I hear you say. Of course, we see from a wider perspective, look into a more highly polished mirror. But who is to say that we are not in many ways as blind as the caterpillar?

In practical terms it is possible (and usually only necessary) to accept the immediate evidence of reality as perceived by the senses; but for the progress of the soul (or the Self, or the 'Real You' or however we describe the essence of ourselves beyond the merely base-level physical) it is necessary to look beyond the momentary and transitory, and gain a perception of the fantastic interweaving interplay of the whole. You have to cultivate what I call 'Paradoxical perception' – the ability to see both the immediate and the ultimate at one and the same time.

Many Zen *Koans* (puzzles) are pathways to reconciling or accepting paradoxes, and sub-nuclear physics gives us practice in coming to terms with twentieth-century paradoxes. One only has to consider light, for example, acting at one time as a wave, and at another as a particle, each being mutually exclusive. This recently emerging branch of science has spelled the end of the total sway of Newtonian physics.

There was a time, not so long ago, when scientists believed that the world – indeed the universe and all the matter it comprised – simply consisted of minute building blocks, atoms; and that if we kept breaking these blocks down further and further, until we could not go any smaller, then we would have in our grasp the ultimate structure of all things, *and we would then know exactly how everything worked!*

Where is that certainty now? We broke the universe down into little blocks, and then we even broke them down further still, and what have we found? It all depends upon our point of view. For example, if we track the motion of a sub-atomic particle we CAN know where it is going, but not how fast! Or, we can discover the speed at which it is travelling, but NOT its direction!

The 'Truth' or 'Reality' then, depends on us, for we must decide what we want to know, and make a choice, because our very decision to test for the truth actually has an effect upon it. Life is actually absolutely fantastic!

Of course, the Newtonian Laws still work as well as ever on the plane of our everyday reality. You can shoot an arrow into the air, measure its speed, and plot exactly where it will go; but these comforting laws simply do not work at the sub-nuclear level.

This being so, every physicist working in this area has had to 'polish the mirror' a little more, and see reality more accurately, even to the extent of learning to live with paradox and a universe which tends to act more like an idea than a thing (to paraphrase – I think – Sir James Jeans).

This, in effect, means learning to live on two distinct levels at the same time, the relative and the absolute. Both co-exist simultaneously, the only difference being that the enlightened man is aware of this duality of view, whereas to the unenlightened what is seen is all there is.

It may appear that by referring to 'Enlightenment' I'm speaking as one who has reached that stage. Far from it! Perhaps I should more properly talk not of Enlightenment, which seems to carry the suggestion of a finished process, but rather of *Zanshin*, a more transient 'Awareness', being the 'unattached' non-discriminating mind applied to a particular subject, object or occasion.

Zanshin is what we strive for when facing an opponent, but it is also what we should aim for in all other areas of life. In my experience this is manifest in a greater (but fluctuating) understanding and perception, which – at my stage of practice of the 'Way' – comes and goes, and is greatly dependent upon circumstances and emotions. This inability of mine to maintain the state at all times I put down to being only partly along the way, and it is only a partial experience of the ultimate state of *Satori*, of which *Zanshin* is one aspect.

The understanding I have of Enlightenment is that it is a little like dealing with the practicalities of existence with the forefront of the mind, whilst setting them into context against the overall, universal picture in the background of the mind. This allows a proper sense of perspective to be maintained, and upsets, tragedies and difficulties assume their correct proportions against an infinite timescale.

Of course, this also means that with this larger-scale view comes acceptance and understanding, not only of the workings of fate and the deeds of others, but of one's own regretted omissions and misdeeds. It becomes possible to forgive oneself for being human!

To quote Dr. Paul Brunton (whose metaphysical works I recommend without reservation):

If we question time and matter – those foundations of all our worldly experience – for their real nature, we come up against . . . paradox and contradiction . . . The only proposition which can properly be affirmed is that they exist and do not exist at the same time.

(*Relatively, Philosophy and Mind*, Larson, p.23)

2 Types of meditation

It would be remiss of me not to point out that there is a technique, which bears some similarity to the types of meditation which I will be discussing, where one induces a state of relaxation by progressively tensing and then relaxing the muscles of the body. This can indeed be beneficial as a stress-reducing exercise, provided that one has the time and a private place suitable for lying down. Effective as this may be, it cannot compare with the efficiency of *Zazen*, for example, at maintaining mental focus and equilibrium after a few deep relaxing breaths, in all situations, provided that one has practised assiduously.

Rinzai and Soto Zen

Zen Buddhism made its reappearance in Japan in 1191 with the return from China of a Japanese priest called Eisai (Senko Kokushi). He was instrumental in establishing a temple at Kamakura and another at Kyoto.[5] Eisai began teaching what was termed *Rinzai* Zen which concentrated upon achieving enlightenment through continual meditation upon *Koans*, sayings or questions which were often paradoxical and were intended to baffle the intellect and force the seeker to go beyond the confines of logical thought and develop a piercing, intuitive understanding of himself and his relationship with the world.

The simplicity of life: praying before eating. No meat, no fish. Reverence for life.

It was this style of Zen that gained the patronage of the Kamakura Shogunate, and became popular with the Samurai warriors. At this time, it was rare for any of the Samurai to have much in the way of literary attainment, so it was difficult to instruct them in the reading of the classical Chinese sutras. So Eisai formulated a number of philosophical puzzles which forced an intuitive 'leap' towards understanding based upon selections from the sutras, and especially suited for warriors and monks.

This process was continued by his successors, and eventually a style of teaching emerged which was based upon the abilities and background of the students, rather than upon the classical knowledge of the master.

There was also the problem that some of the Zen masters – Daikaku for example – had at that time a very poor command of the Japanese

Seizing the moment! No thoughts of victory or defeat, a strong will and complete concentration, then total commitment.

Buddhist monks in meditation.

The Golden Pavilion, built by Ashikaga Yoshimitsu in
1397. A monument to the culture of the age.

The Roan-ji Temple, Kyoto. The tranquility of the Zen
Rock Garden.

language. Thus it was necessary to devise a system based upon few words but of dramatic impact.

The Kamakura Samurai were expected to be prepared to die at an instant's notice, and the immediacy and directness of this type of Zen, emphasising self-reliance, the transient nature of all things, the need to pierce the clouds of illusion for a true appreciation of reality, had a strong attraction. Naturally, these same qualities did not go unnoticed by the ruling classes, who saw in it, as well as the ennobling elements, characteristics which would make it a pretty good tool for the state.

Of course, it was not just Zen that encouraged the rise of the Samurai as extremely efficient, unafraid warriors; there were also the combined influences of *Shinto* and *Confucianism* (which I describe elsewhere[6]). But it was through the meditational practices introduced by Zen that their psychological approach to combat was refined.

There was another type of Zen which was introduced into Japan somewhat later by Dogen (1200–1253) who was also a Japanese priest who had gone to study in China. This was *Soto* Zen, in which the emphasis lay in sitting in *Zazen*, in a cross-legged posture, and carrying out practices to still the logical mind and entering a state of non-discriminatory awareness.

Little need was felt for the more forceful questioning; just sitting was enough. Letting go of thought, desire, needs and ambitions, and simply allowing the 'Original Face' to be revealed, would be to gain enlightenment, and thus freedom from the pressures and fears of the flesh.

Of the two kinds, it was the directness of *Rinzai* Zen that held sway with the warrior class.

Transcendental meditation

Technically there is little difference between the physical characteristics of this twentieth-century meditational system and that of *Zazen*. The physiological changes brought about by practice also vary little from those developed in the traditional Eastern kinds. All emphasise the need for the meditator to assume an erect posture, allowing breathing to be deep and easy, and for the subject to be able to enter a state of relaxed awareness.

TM, however, acknowledges the characteristic of a society unused to squatting on the ground, and allows the use of a chair for the meditator (not, of course, that Zen cannot be practised in any position, but normally one sits crossed-legged on a cushion). Rather than just sitting – as in *Soto* Zen – or in working on a *Koan* – as in *Rinzai* – the meditator is given a personal mantra to hold in the mind and to vocalise as a meaningless sound, not to think about or to concentrate on, but to serve as a point upon which the consciousness can initially rest before reaching even more subtle levels. As in *Soto* Zen, there should be effortless attention, no forcing of the mind.

TM normally advocates meditation in two daily 20-minute periods.

One cannot see into the depths of a lake unless the surface of the water is still and calm.

(Maharishi Mahesh Yogi)

All the systems are based on the understanding that there is a fundamental unity underlying all things, and they emphasise the need to develop the ability to transcend the mundane appearance of the world by increasing awareness and eliminating illusory thinking through stilling the frantic activity of the mind's concern over everyday trivialities.

As far as the martial artist is concerned, I see no difference between any of the systems if we are simply seeking the physiological benefits of the relaxation response.

To achieve the concomitant of *Zanshin*, however, it really is vital that we come to grips with the problems of our fears and reactions to them which arise through our incomplete view of the world. For me, then, there is no system that I can recommend if the practice does not include introspection, contemplation and an eventual achievement of what I believe to be a truer concept of reality.

By a continual mixture of the pure awareness of *Soto* meditation, and what I call the '*Rinzai-type*', wherein one either fiercely struggles with a concept, or gently lets it permeate one's consciousness, it is possible to develop the ability to cut through and reconcile the apparent dualistic nature of reality and to arrive at my 'paradoxical perception'.

This should lead to a greater awareness of the human condition, and with it a sense of understanding and compassion, and a propensity for Good rather than Evil. This 'awareness', and the mental toughness which stems from the concentration and discipline of meditation practice, should then be applied in a similar way during your physical martial training.

This will lead to the state of *Mizu no Kokoro* ('Mind like Water'), unemotional, reflecting all but getting 'hung up' on nothing; concentrating not on defeat, nor on victory, just total, undiscriminating concentration. In a word, *Zanshin*.[7]

3 The historical evidence

Most of the Samurai were followers of the Japanese national religion. *Shinto*, the principal tenet being that everything in nature was imbued with a form of spirit *(Shin)*. As we have seen, they developed a strong inclination towards the simplicity and directness of the form of Buddhism known as *Zen (Cha'an* in Chinese).

To the warrior, the emphasis on self-control and complete awareness combined with a philosophy which inculcated calmness and tranquillity even in the face of death was irresistible. Living and dying was, for them, balanced on the stroke of a sword, in a society whose ethos demanded swift and violent response to a vast range of transgressions.

This was a culture which honoured the priest and appreciated the poet, but at the same time could slay a commoner without compunction for not bowing quickly enough.

It was an age wherein it was possible for a Samurai of good status to enjoy art, a comfortable family life, the tea-house, the Willow World and all the trappings and privileges of office, but upon an instant he might be forced to cut open his own belly at the word of his feudal lord! In this milieu, *Zen* with its resolution of paradox, was understandably attractive.

Moreover in his daily meditative practice the Samurai could actually find the harmony and one-ness beneath the chaos, and turn the sharpening of the intuitive response which it developed into a tool for making his combat more effective.

He also came to understand the transitory nature of all things, and thus came to terms with his own mortality. Fear of dying then gave way to acceptance, from which developed the primary concern which was to make the inevitable a meaningful act, rather than an ignoble occurrence.

The meditation of the Samurai, was aimed at more than just inculcating a passive acceptance of dying, and although often falling short of the mark, it could lead to examples of almost unimaginable coolness and presence of mind in the most dire circumstances. It became the custom, for example, for a warrior resolved to take his own life to compose a Death Poem, exemplifying his unwavering strength of spirit, even faced with *Seppuku* (*Hara-Kiri* – 'Belly-cutting') a horrifyingly painful and self-inflicted way of death.

The author, evidence of the severity of the early training.

The suicide of the seventy-four-year-old warrior, Yorimasa Minamoto, in the Gempei War (1180–1185) is characteristic. With his defences failing under the onslaught of the Taira warriors, and with both sons and himself wounded, he composed his farewell poem and wrote it upon the back of his war-fan:

> Like a fossil tree from which we gather no flowers
> Sad has been my life, fated to produce no fruit!

He then ripped open his belly with his short sword and died.

Zen meditation also aimed at developing the intuitive response, rather than the purely deductive and rational. This led the Samurai towards an approach to combat that stressed the importance of seizing the opportunity to strike, of concentrating all of mind, technique and spirit into one split-second of total commitment.

Single combat, even among armies drawn up on the field of battle, was often a formal affair. Names, ranks and lineage were announced, and care taken that witnesses were present to record the event. Much emphasis was placed upon the deliberate taking of positions and the unhurried assessment of each other's style, strengths and weaknesses. Then, quick as a flash, with one stroke it was over. One – and sometimes both – of the protagonists would lie dead: *Ai-uchi!*

It was essential, then, to be able to seize an opening on the instant, without conscious thought. It was not possible to take the time to think about which technique to use, which block, which counter-strike. Those milliseconds of indecision would mean extinction.

In many *Dojos* nowadays this intensity of experience is lost. One might say: 'And naturally so', as the training no longer leads to battlefield encounters, and fights are for points rather than lives. Again, the rise in the popularity of 'Sport' karate, 'Sport' judo, and the like, encourages the move away from the need for such intensity.

Matches are for points only, not lives; a referee is on hand to make sure that none of the combatants is badly injured. The worst injuries are through accident rather than by intention, and are seldom very serious.

Unfortunately this also leads inexorably away from the refining and development of *Zanshin* and from practice in dealing appropriately

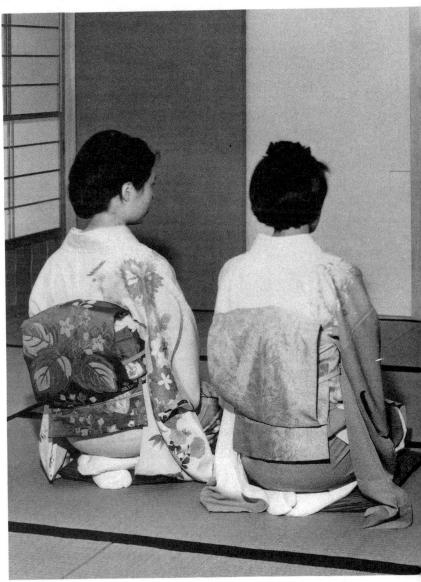

*The Tea Ceremony: Zen in ordinary life. The quiet, calm
appreciation of 'Now!' The complete absorption with the
present moment.*

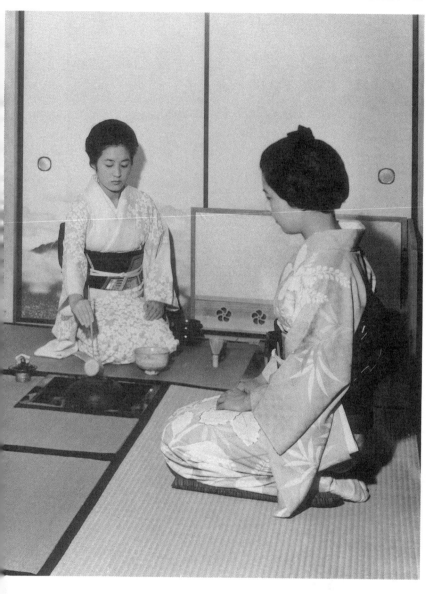

Shiro Asano, on his arrival in England.

The Honbu team, Vince second right. Note (as usual) the co-opted fifth man. Bottom: Another championship, this time only three black-belts. Vince far right. Note evidence of the severity of early championships!

*Honbu line-up for a demonstration. (Note Aidan Trimble
third left, and Vince, next to Asano sensei, second right.)*

*Student and Master. A delighted Vince receives a medal
from Asano sensei.*

with life-or-death situations. Even in 'traditional' Dojos the training is by no means as severe as it was twenty or so years ago when I first met Asano sensei, who was to be my teacher for many years.

I will not presume to bore you with reminiscences, but it is worth making the point that to Asano sensei there was no such concept as 'Sport' karate. His regime was so severe that for many of the years that I was one of his senior students there was only a core of about four high grades who continued – day in, day out – to endure the harshness (although many would come and go from time to time).

Asano had been captain of the renowned Takushoku University Dojo, (now closed owing to the severity of its training regime) and twice the all-Japan students' champion. He was from an old Samurai

With Sode sensei, who introduced Vince to Atama-ate *in Kumite. Note the sweat-soaked Gi!*

family, and had established a reputation at the Japan Karate Association Honbu as a fearsome and cunning fighter with a liking for *Mawashi-geri* ('roundhouse kicks').

Sensei's training was centred entirely on the traditional way, of concentrating upon the developing of a strong spirit, with no thought, for example, for tomorrow. Only the present moment was important, and had to be experienced to the full.

This led to sparring sessions with him, and with the other senior students, every training session, which were really mini-wars. Of course we pulled our techniques somewhat to the head, but the body was considered fair game. No techniques were forbidden, and I well remember being introduced to the art of head-butting in *ju-kumite* with another JKA instructor who was assisting Mr. Asano at the time, Mr. Sode.

Over the years of training, teeth were knocked out, ribs broken, tendons snapped and black eyes common. In fact, the very first time I ever met Asano sensei (I think I was about 4th Kyu at the time) he called me out for sparring and promptly knocked me unconscious with a *Jodan mawashi-geri*. When I came round I found that some of the other students had carried me into the changing rooms to hold my head under the cold tap. I had to carry on the rest of the training session with only one eye open. (It was a week before the other opened up!)

This regime carried on for many years, and I could give many similar examples. The point that I want to stress, however, is that this type of training was as near as it was possible to get to establishing the feeling of life-or-death encounters, and I really do mean this.

Of course, not every sparring partner was out to kill or maim you, nor would they all have had the skill. None the less, during every session it was usual to fight with at least one or two who either had no control, or who didn't believe in it, or who simply weren't concerned with the niceties of protocol such as acknowledging a good technique or a successful counter, but who were not content until they had put their opponent on his back. And we had to fight Asano sensei as well! Not to mention a continual stream of visiting junior and senior JKA instructors who came to pay their respects to sensei before taking up posts in Europe.

My last example (for now anyway) to illuminate the intensity of the training is as follows. Sensei knew that I suffered quite severely from asthma, and his fights with me became almost legendary – not because of the brilliance of my technique, let me quickly say (how I wish it were!). No. Although he fought all the seniors he invariably kept me out far longer than any of them, and, naturally, after a certain time I would develop great difficulty in breathing. At this stage, you would imagine that he would recognise this and allow me to sit down.

Not at all! At this stage he would begin to press me even harder, until I really couldn't breathe, then he would knock me down. Each time I struggled to my feet he would knock me down or sweep me again.

I can remember seeing out of the corner of my eye, as I got back to my feet, some of the other class members, who would all be seated in a line at the edge of the area. They knew that I wouldn't give in, and they also knew that I was too far gone to fight back, so they would turn their heads away, not really wanting to be a part of this apparent brutality.

The moment actually came in one particular fight that will stay with me for ever, the moment when I thought that I was going to die! My mind, inside my exhausted body, was quite calm, and almost a disinterested observer of my fighting to breathe and to get up again. I knew that I could end this pain at any time by simply staying on the floor.

I also knew if I did this I would have admitted to defeat. Not of skill – Sensei was already my master there – but in a very personal way, in that I felt that I would be surrendering to my own weaknesses. I found, at that profound level, that I could quite coldly and calmly make the decision to die.

I looked up and saw Sensei just looking at me, waiting. So, I made my decision and my mind – almost ludicrously – quite cheerfully thought: 'You might beat my body, but you can't beat me!' and seeing the funny side: 'How will you explain away my body then?'

I struggled to my feet, and I couldn't even raise my fists or attempt any sort of guard. My chest and lungs felt as if they were bursting with the effort to drag oxygen into them. It was just how it must feel to drown! Still Sensei stood there.

Not able to take any stance or guard I just resolved to try and knock him over by charging at him. I launched my attack and also launched myself into what I expected to be my last moments in this existence. My attack was a joke! All I could do was stumble and stagger forward.

At that instant, for the first time in all the years of battles I had with Sensei, he stopped me, said 'Oss!' and motioned me to sit down. So I had died, yet not died!

I ramble on; but to me this was a deeply significant stage in my training, and in retrospect I can see that it was in these highly intense moments that Sensei was keeping us in the tradition of the true martial arts in order to develop the strength of our spirits by forging them in the same fires as the Samurai of old.

Training today, even in my Dojo, is different. Perhaps rightly so, but if the martial arts are ever to be more than just sports a conscious attempt must be made in every Dojo to develop a training system which, if not so brutal, must force the students continually to face up to their fears and weaknesses in order to travel beyond them.

Without danger there can be no need for *Zanshin*. If a watered-down martial art does not require *Zanshin*, and doesn't develop it, then it is no longer any different from any other sport which demands great concentration and physical effort.

I do believe, however, that it is possible to foster the development of *Zanshin* in the modern Dojo, but it does mean that the Sensei must take on the responsibility of devising training methods – at least for the higher grades – which place tremendous demands upon them, and should also guide them in their meditation practices. I will say, quite bluntly, that if neither aspect is catered for, then that Dojo is not practising a martial art, and the students will never realise their full potential, because the 'Way' doesn't lead anywhere!

What I can promise you, and there is no doubt in my mind about this, as my own personal experiences will testify, is this: if you persist in regular practice of Karate in the traditional fashion that I have described, and if you also follow a regular pattern of meditation (both the *Soto* or relaxation type and the contemplative, searching *Rinzai* type) you will find that you will face life differently. The strong spirit that buoys you up when facing a dangerous foe will also serve you well when dealing with other pressing problems of life.

You will act with a new confidence, assured that your actions are now based upon a wider view of the various interweaving strands of reality. You will find that you will psychologically be far better able to deal with the stresses of daily life, and you will be physically more prepared to aid your immune system in maintaining the body's natural balance and thus fight off illness. Why not try it?

One word of caution, however. Meditation is not a light switch. You cannot just switch it on, and expect it to work. It is a cumulative, progressive process, and therefore you must allow yourself at least a month or so before you really start to appreciate all the benefits. Set yourself a simple goal of perhaps only 20 minutes a day to begin with – either in one period, or two periods of 10 minutes.

I also advise you to alternate the type of meditation, starting with just sitting and counting your breaths to still the mind. When you can do this successfully then move on to selecting a topic (perhaps a paragraph from one of Paul Brunton's Notebooks, which are ideal for this; or perhaps one of the traditional Zen *Koans*) and spend your meditation gently looking at it from all angles until the time is up. Do not place any expectations upon this. Just look. Insights will arise when you are ready to receive them.

I discovered that the way of the Samurai is Death. In a fifty-fifty life or death crisis, simply settle it by choosing immediate death. There is nothing complicated about it. Just brace yourself and proceed.

(*Hagakure* – Book 1)

People who do not want to follow the teaching of Zen, the true foundation of Budo, do not have to do so. They're simply using the martial arts as playthings; to them they are sports like any others.

But people who want to live their lives on a higher dimension do have to understand.

. . . The teachers are partly responsible for this state of affairs; they train the body and teach technique, but do nothing for the conscious-ness. As a result their pupils fight to win. Like children playing war games. There is no wisdom in this approach, and it is no use at all in . . . managing one's life.

(*Taisen Deshimaru*)

During the practice you should imagine you are on the battlefield. When blocking and striking make the eyes glare, drop the shoulders and harden the body. Now block the enemy's punch and strike! *Always practise with this spirit* so that when on the real battlefield, you will naturally be prepared.

(Anko Itosu)

Since karate is a martial art, you must practise with the utmost seriousness from the very beginning. This means going beyond being simply diligent in your training. In every step, in every movement of your hand, you must imagine yourself facing an opponent with a drawn sword.

Each and every punch must be made with the power of your entire body behind it, with the feeling of destroying your opponent with a single blow. You must believe that if your punch fails, you will forfeit your own life. Thinking this your mind and energy will be concentrated, and your spirit will express itself to the fullest.

No matter how much time you devote to practice, no matter how many months or years pass, if your practice consists of no more than moving your arms and legs, you might as well be studying dance. You will never come to know the true meaning of karate.

(Gichin Funakoshi)

4 The contemporary evidence

In the last few years a lot of research has been carried out into the effects of meditation upon athletic performance. One of the common results has been to show that a harmonisation occurs between the higher and lower brain centres, and between the left and right hemispheres.

The importance to athletes of this evidence is that, as I have noted earlier, it seems that the left hemisphere is the centre of the logical, reasoning part of Man, involved in dealing with abstract thinking, mathematics, language and the like; whereas the right hemisphere is more involved in the intuitive, musical and artistic functions. This right side is also apparently the centre of skills to do with spatial awareness, kinesthesis and motor adjustments connected with spatial awareness.

Research has shown that righthanded people have the seat of control of their dominant side in the left hemisphere. In lefthanded people the centre of control is in the right side of the brain. It is interesting to note that several top ball players (Jimmy Connors, Rod Laver, John McEnroe, Martina Navratilova, for example) are lefthanded. This indicates a greater right hemisphere influence, and thus the probability of greater degree of spatial awareness and the ability to physically adjust to this awareness.

Some researchers, realising this, have advocated that it is worthwhile for – say – righthanded (and thus left-brain-dominant) athletes to practise favouring the left hand and foot for a while, so as to enhance their creativity by forcing the right brain into greater activity.

The aim of this type of exercise would be to promote a greater degree of harmonisation and integration between both halves of the brain. *This is exactly what meditation achieves!*

The author.

In practice, taking evidence from a carefully designed study of a group of athletes beginning a programme of Transcendental Meditation, it was found that after splitting the group into two, with half meditating for 20 minutes twice a day and the other half spending the same time relaxing with eyes closed, all of the meditating group improved significantly over a whole range of physical tests in comparison with the non-meditators.

The researchers concluded that TM helped the athletes to develop a broad range of qualifications essential to their performance, including specific attributes such as speed, endurance, agility, faster reactions and better mind-body co-ordination.

5 How to meditate

This section gives you a step-by-step introduction to basic meditation beginning with the relaxation type, and moving on to learning techniques of stilling the mind. From here we go on to look at ways to improve concentration, and then to suggestions for quiet contemplation. Once the basics are mastered you can then go on to use specific visualisation techniques aimed at improving your own martial skills, and I will be giving some examples of how this may be done.

Traditionally, the best times to meditate were considered to be at sunrise and sunset. I well remember my own struggles to attend 4 a.m. Zen meditation practices, not to mention the feeling of Chiba Roshi's *Kyosaku* across my shoulders when my attention wavered!

You, however, are the best person to decide when it will be most convenient for you. What is important, though, is that you do *make time* for regular practice. Give yourself a chance. This practice is meant to continue even when the first fires of enthusiasm have died down. So don't choose times which will be difficult for you to keep to.

Don't forget: you will need to follow a regular pattern of meditation over a period for the results to become apparent. Just as in your martial arts training, it takes time for your body to assimilate the new and unfamiliar demands.

As for how long? Well, there's little point in starting out on a regime which you will soon tire of and allow to lapse. Initially, then, I suggest that you allot yourself only 15 to 20 minutes a day in order to become accustomed to the techniques. This is surely not too much time for you to afford! After a week or two you should then increase the time to 30 minutes daily.

Of course, the time spent will, to a large extent, be governed by the type of meditation you are practising. The relaxation type, for instance, will never really require more than about 20 minutes or so to be effective. The other types will need a little longer. As it happens, you will not find this to be anything of an imposition, and you will find yourself actually looking forward to these few moments of peace in an otherwise busy day.

One point, however, to those who will be thinking: 'Well, why not just have a cat-nap instead of meditating, surely that will relax me?' The fact is, that research shows conclusively that the levels of relaxation during meditation, and the results arising, are of a far more profound order than those during and accruing from sleep, or from simply sitting quietly with your mind engaged in activities such as reading or watching the television.

The evidence demonstrates physiological changes in brain electrical activity, a decrease in muscle tonus, a reduction in blood lactate levels, and so on, indicating an observable decrease in the activity of the sympathetic nervous system.

So, you have the time, now you must select the right place. You should find somewhere where you can be reasonably sure that you will not be disturbed – hang a sign on the door as well! It should be quiet, and dimly lit, and you will find it advantageous to wear fairly loose-fitting clothes. You will also need a firm cushion to support the buttocks (traditionally called a *Zafu*). Do not try to meditate too soon after a meal, or bodily functions may act as a distraction.

The traditional meditation schools insist that unless there is a good reason one should assume a cross-legged seated position, either full or half lotus, with the head reaching for the sky and the knees pressing into the earth. Most people can gain at least the tailor's cross-legged position, even if this does cause some initial discomfort. Like anything else, you have to practise, little and often.

Should you suffer from some disability which precludes these positions, then perhaps the kneeling *Mokuso* configuration, with the *Zafu* held between the knees as a support for the buttocks will be a reasonable alternative which will still enable you to maintain the basic upright spine. If none of these is possible, then simply sit upright in a highbacked dining chair.

Whichever position you choose, you should sit upright, with your nose directly in line with your sternum. Tuck your chin in slightly, and hold your head as if someone were pulling upwards on the top. Whilst once again there are traditionally recommended ways of holding the hands, in my experience simplicity should be paramount; therefore just place the palms of the hands lightly on the tops of your thighs. Just remember to check that you do not have your elbows sticking out.

Upon first getting into position, sway your body slightly forwards and backwards two or three times, gradually bringing it to rest in a vertically erect position. (During your initial practice you should keep checking from time to time to make sure that you are keeping the spine straight.) You should either keep your eyes lightly closed, or half-open, with your gaze somewhat unfocussed downwards some four or five feet in front of you.

When you have established the correct position, take a few deep breaths, and let them out again slowly. As you breathe out allow your body to lose its tension. As you do this, watch the way that your stomach swells and deflates upon each inspiration and exhalation. This is correct, as you should be using diaphragmatic breathing, not upper-body or chest breathing.

At this stage it is important that you do not start to impose stress upon yourself by forcing your breaths into any particular rhythm; just sit quietly until your body establishes its own pattern. By this time you will already be a few minutes into your allotted time, and your breathing will have become slow and regular.

Now allow your attention to follow your breathing pattern and start to count each time that you exhale. 'One' on the first, 'two' on the second, and so on. Continue this until you reach the count of ten. Now start again at 'One'.

I can almost hear the cries of 'Easy!' But it isn't! The aim of this practice is twofold. It helps to further establish the meditational

Meditation is often carried out facing a wall to remove visual stimulation. (Note head monk with Kyosaku, used to strike the shoulders to refocus attention.)

posture and rhythms of breathing, and it can also serve – if done without forcing – to calm the activity of the mind. You will find that it will be difficult to keep your attention solely upon the count. All sorts of other thoughts will bubble up to distract you. You will suddenly find that for the last few moments you have been thinking of something else entirely! *Do NOT get cross with yourself!* After all, this is not an easy discipline. We are trying to get the body and mind into a state of relaxed awareness.

I sometimes ask my students if they relax. They invariably say yes! Then I ask them to describe their relaxation: Tennis, Football, Reading, Listening to music, Sex, Eating, Watching Television and so on. Not one says that they sit still and genuinely relax both body and mind in harmony! They simply exchange one sort of activity (work) for another (leisure).

So, naturally, your mind will find it very difficult to maintain its gentle focus upon such a simple task. Nevertheless, whenever other thoughts arise do not force them away, rather note their passing and refocus upon your breathing . . . 'One. . . . two . . .'

There is another technique which you could try if you cannot get on with counting your breaths, and that is to focus your mind upon an imaginary burning candle. See it in your mind, and watch the flame as it flares and flutters, and the wax as it slowly melts from the top. Watch the colours as they change in the flickering overall glow. Try to maintain this for the next few minutes.

You should realise that if you cannot find the calm stillness in your centre when you are in ideal conditions of quiet and solitude, then you cannot expect to find it in moments of stress!

Eventually you will find that you can successfully continue these exercises without major distractions. When this stage arrives, simply stop counting or concentrating on anything at all. Just watch. Become a detached, disinterested observer – aware of everything and nothing. If noises register upon your hearing do not suddenly begin thinking about them and identifying them; let them go. If a thought occurs to you, do not follow it, nor force it away; let it go. Let it go! Just *be*.

Now you have entered the realms of *Soto* Zen, wherein *Zazen*, just sitting and being, is a state of extraordinary stillness, of one-ness with the universe. Breathing has slowed right down, and almost seems non-existent. One simply *is*.

At this stage encephalographic measurements would show a preponderance of Alpha-wave activity (8–14 cycles per second) and of Theta rhythms (4–7 cycles per second) indicative of a state of deep meditation which is conducive to creative insight and intuitive understanding. Naturally, all the physiological benefits of the relaxation type practice would also manifest themselves.

After some weeks you will find that you will be able to dispense with the initial breath-counting, and enter straight away into the *Zazen* state. You will be able to 'switch it on' at will. At this point I would advise that you begin to include some time in your meditation practice devoted to contemplation of what – to me – are the most important considerations that exist.

Sometimes you can use this state of creative awareness to reach sudden flashes of illumination, like the sun suddenly breaking through to light up a landscape. Sometimes you can struggle and chew on a thought like a terrier with a bone until you reach the marrow. You will find that you will expand your mind and awareness to comprehend the whole of the human condition, and it will sometimes move you to tears of compassion. Other insights into your own strengths and weaknesses will prompt you into taking steps to accept your own failings and then to try and rectify them.

I recommend that you read a little of the Buddhist literature. (But don't fall into the trap of thinking that any amount of reading will generate any of the benefits of meditation. You cannot get the taste of a cup of tea by reading about it – you actually have to drink it!) From these sources I suggest you take a couple of sentences which strike a chord in your mind, and just let the play of your mind shake them about, turn them inside and out, and generally look at them from every angle.

As a matter of interest you may like to take a look at some of the note-books of Dr Paul Brunton. These are helpful not solely for their exceptionally enlightened content, but in that they are presented in convenient paragraphs which are perfect for meditation.

Remember that the ultimate purpose of meditation is not to enhance one's fighting skills, although it has been found to do that, but it is rather to help each meditator to transcend the illusory appertainances of the everyday world and to stimulate personal growth in the higher aspects of the psyche. To help this, you should really set some time aside for exposure to spiritually uplifting things: fine paintings, good music, poetry and so on.

A word to male readers: don't be mistaken, there is nothing remotely 'unmanly' about this. The Elizabethan Heroic figure or Complete Man was expected to be not just a courageous soldier, but also a civilised courtier, a poet, a romantic lover and a good husband.

> Even a samurai of low rank should be knowledgable about the art of poetry, and able to compose a verse himself, even though it might well be undistinguished.
>
> (Daidoji Yuzan on *Bushido*)

There has been much written about Buddhism, and Zen in particular, and many writings of the ancient masters have been made available to us. It is often the case, however, that we do not have much time available to us for the luxury of studying what are sometimes very difficult texts in the depth necessary to gain a proper understanding of them.

More often than not, these texts are based on traditions which are quite alien to us, and make allusions to references which may well be immediately recognisable to someone steeped in the history, traditions and background of Eastern religions, but are completely foreign to our Western experience.

It long ago occurred to me that for a philosophy to be relevant to Western Man it should be accessible from within the Western experience. After all, if such a philosophy really has got something to say to all men, then it should be understandable to all men.

From my experience as a Medieval scholar, with a particular interest in the literature and background of the Anglo-Saxon and the Old Norse societies, I have continually been made aware that – no matter what age we consider – there is a continuous underlying theme of Man attempting to rise above human frailty; often struggling heroically against tremendous odds. Many instances can be shown of enormous courage and self-sacrifice, often in quite hopeless situations, where the strength of the human spirit shines like a beacon, growing even stronger in the face of an unavoidable end.

There is no need to think that the courage to face death unflinchingly and heroically was only available to the Samurai. Nor is there reason to believe that only the cultures of the East could emphasise the cultivation of a civilised and noble way of life, and the concept of honour and duty, alongside the cult of the warrior.

Far from it! Look at the Battle of Thermopylae. In the year 480 BC, the Persian army of some 180,000 warriors under the command of Xerxes attempted to invade Greece, but were held at the narrow pass of Thermopylae by a small force of 300 heroic Spartans led by Leonidas. The epic deeds of this small force allowed the Greek army to retreat and re-form, and ultimately to throw back the invaders; and the whole world is aware of the debts that are owed to what has been termed the seat of Western Civilisation.

Read 'The Battle of Maldon', a poetic account of Anglo-Saxon heroism in the face of Viking invasion in the year 991, wherein many similarities with the Samurai can be noted. The Anglo-Saxon

Mokuso.

Comitatus, or members of the Feudal Lord's war band, were directly comparable in status and duties to their Japanese counterparts, and their courage, loyalty and spirit, and even their practice of announcing their lineage on the battlefield before engaging in heroic deeds of single combat exactly echoes that of the Samurai. Their creed was simply stated:

May our spirit grow stronger, our hearts grow keener and our courage greater as our strength grows less!

One of the lasting mementos of the Anglo-Saxon period is their obvious love of poetry, especially that extolling the deeds of heroes, and also elegiac verse full of a pervading sorrow for the transience of all mortal things.

Later, from French and Italian Romance traditions of the noble Roland, (one of the great Charlemagne's generals) to the knightly epics of the *Morte D'Arthur* and British Arthurian legend, literature abounds in stories of the deeds of selfless warriors, whose avowed intent was to be fearless in the face of overwhelming odds, and to devote their lives to the discovery of the Holy Grail – a potent symbol of Justice and Love and the highest qualities of spirit.

However, it was during my studies that I first came across the work of Rudyard Kipling, who, although perhaps best known for *The Jungle Book* and *The Just So Stories*, was also a strong and perceptive poet and balladeer. It was upon reading his poem 'If' that I realised that here was a work, albeit written by a man born and raised in India and who had much knowledge of Eastern Philosophy, that was couched directly in terms which made it immediately comprehensible to the Western reader.

The longer I considered the poem the more I came to see that it was almost the perfect encapsulation of the same Zen concerns of the *Koans*, and of the self-transcending philosophy which lay behind the *Bushido* ethic. This made it an ideal vehicle for meditational contemplation.

6 'If'

I will first give the poem in full, then spend a little time discussing some of the passages and indicating the directions in which contemplation of a number of its statements led me. Naturally, I hope that you will make the effort to think about some of these points for yourself during your meditation.

Do choose small segments, and first think about what is immediately obvious, that is, the literal statement. Then – remembering that it is a poem after all – do try to gain an overall feeling from the work. Then just sit quietly in your chosen meditation posture, and allow your mind to reflect upon the selected passage. Set it in its context, as a piece of advice, which is offered for someone to listen to and take heed of. How true is it, in your experience? Do any of the points strike a chord in your mind? Do any apply to you? Can you think of any situations which, had you been able to carry out this advice, would have turned out more satisfactorily? Do you disagree with any statements or advice, and if so, why? And so on.

> If you can keep your head when all about you
>   Are losing theirs and blaming it on you.
> If you can trust yourself when all men doubt you,
>   But make allowance for their doubting too;

If you can wait and not be tired by waiting,
  Or being lied about, don't deal in lies,
Or being hated, don't give way to hating,
  And yet don't look too good, nor talk too wise;

If you can dream – and not make dreams your master;
  If you can think – and not make thoughts your aim;
If you can meet with Triumph and Disaster
  And treat those two impostors just the same;
If you can bear to hear the truth you've spoken
  Twisted by knaves to make a trap for fools,
Or watch the things you gave your life to, broken,
  And stoop and build 'em up with worn-out tools;

If you can make one heap of all your winnings
  And risk it on one turn of pitch-and-toss,
And lose, and start again at your beginnings
  And never breathe a word about your loss;
If you can force your heart and nerve and sinew
  To serve your turn long after they are gone,
And so hold on when there is nothing in you
  Except the Will which says to them: 'Hold on!'

If you can talk with crowds and keep your virtue,
  Or walk with Kings – nor lose the common touch,
If neither foes nor loving friends can hurt you,
  If all men count with you, but none too much;
If you can fill the unforgiving minute
  With sixty seconds' worth of distance run,
Yours is the Earth and everything that's in it,
  And – which is more – you'll be a Man, my son.

'If' by Rudyard Kipling.

Let's begin by looking at just the first verse. What are the qualities that are being advocated? 'Keeping your head'? Yes, that's pretty obviously a good characteristic: keeping cool in a crisis. But here it's even more, for you are being blamed for the crisis! Maybe it's your fault, maybe not, but do you lose your temper when things go wrong, even if it is your fault? If you do, does it help or could you perhaps have achieved more by retaining control?

How cool do you keep when facing a powerful adversary in the Dojo, or how level-headed when someone steals your parking place? Think of a few situations which are applicable to you, and run them through in your head with you acting in a more rational manner. In a crisis, an accident or a disaster, would your panic reaction be helpful or unhelpful?[8]

O.K.: 'Trust yourself when all men doubt you, *but make allowance for their doubting.*' Can you handle the stresses of decision-making, especially when others think you wrong? Can you live without the approbation of your peers? Can you still make the *right* decision when under pressure, or are you influenced by the desire to look good in the eyes of others?

Can you understand people who do not agree with you, or do you dismiss them as obviously wrong-headed? Are you able to make allowances for doubters, and help them towards understanding, or do you drag them along because you are the boss, or because it is better for them, and you know best?

Have you got patience? The Japanese had a saying: 'Be knocked down seven times, get up eight!' The Scots: 'If at first you don't succeed, try, try again!' Obviously a common concept, but to a martial artist, surely something more? After all, we are practising for perfection. How long are you prepared to wait, or do you really expect to achieve it some day? How many months, how many years, how many lifetimes?

In confrontation or combat, do you have the patience to wait, or will you eventually, feeling that you *must* do something, act rashly, and be cut down? In helping, how many times before you wash your hands of the situation and say: 'Well, I did try!' In meditation, are you eager for results? Too eager? What results?

Let's go on to look at the questions raised by 'Lies'. What lies? The obvious untruths. Or the more subtle excuses that *we* make for our own weaknesses? The problem with lying is that it obscures the truth! The antithesis of all martial and meditative practice!

'Look . . . good . . . talk too wise.' How proud are you, how much pleasure does status or power give to you, to your Ego? The emphasis is upon the external appearance of things, which is most often not at all the reality. How can you 'talk *too* wise'? It is not what you say, but rather the manner in which you say it. Do not study to give the appearance of wisdom (nor anything), for wisdom will speak for itself, with no accretions of outward display.

Do not seek to set yourself above the rest, and certainly do not think that your achievements or accomplishments mark you out as better. Two people, one 6ft tall, the other 5ft 5ins.: which is better? Two athletes, both train to the very utmost of their being; they race, one wins. Which is better?

You can – and should – try to be the sort of person to whom others can turn for help or advice, or direction; but this is just for the love of fellow man, not for any surplus illusory baggage of pride.

Moving on to the second verse, let's consider the first two lines. Yes, dream, but don't go through life as a dreamer; be a thoughtful person, but not at the expense of action. For thinking on its own cannot change anything. The thought must 'Be the father to the deed'.

And now, the lines which should be required reading for every competitive karate-ka. What does it mean, that 'Disaster' and 'Triumph' are impostors? In Zen terms, they are both unreal in that they are illusions. What really is success and what is failure? To win a Championship Title is marvellous, and a fitting reward for great periods of practice and concentrated effort. But what does it really signify? That you are the best? Best what? Competition fighter? Hardly, for there are probably better fighters somewhere in the world, or there were, or will be. Best in courage and commitment? Well, what about the fighter that came second? Best in technique? No 'lucky' decisions by the referee? . . . And so on.

Please don't think that I am belittling champions; far from it. I am still proud of my own little collection of cups, trophies and awards. What matters is that these things are seen for what they really are, freeze-frame snapshots of a fleeting moment in your life. If the medals serve to encourage you to continue to approach all of your life with as much zest and effort – fine! Just don't get tied down in hunting trophies to feed your Ego. Win them, then put them away.

Now turn all this on its head, and apply it equally harshly to the concept of failure or 'Disaster'. What does it mean, wherein lies failure? Surely not in trying for something which doesn't come off? What is the ultimate disaster. Death? Well, that will come as it may, and who is to say whether or not we can rightly term that Disaster? Anything less gives us further opportunity for growing in so many ways, and is there nothing positive which can serve to help us in future situations that we can learn from what we are now experiencing? What you should do is let go. Let go of the illusory aspects of both triumph and disaster and move on. This verse is trying to make us see the importance of what we know as the martial spirit. Never give in, no matter what, and no matter how tired or weary we may be. We must pick up our 'worn-out tools' and start again. Final success is not the goal. That may or may not arrive; but we must continue to strive along the way.

Perseverance and the nerve to make total commitment to a task are the underlying concept in verse 3: spirit and courage in the face of adversity; whilst the last verse stresses integrity and personal honour, as well as exhorting us to live in the NOW of life, to waste no precious moments nor to wish our time away.

We must make use of here and now. Time, we know, is relative, and is inextricably interwoven with space. It can expand or contract, dependent upon a number of factors. We know that if space travellers could travel at speeds approaching that of light, time for them would pass at a different rate than for those of us left behind here on Earth.

The poem underlines, however, that for all of us time is 'unforgiving'. What we should do, we should do now! And who will forgive us if we waste our chances? For the Samurai, there was the ever-present reminder that one day — perhaps this day – time would run out. Zen and Buddhist sutras continually emphasised the 'Nowness' of existence; so does this poem!

'You'll be a Man, my son!' The final statement makes us think about all that the idea of 'Man' involves – the qualities, the weaknesses, the aspirations to nobility on the one hand, the degradations of the torturer on the other. Think deeply about what it does and doesn't mean; what the concept signifies to you.

So, you can get some idea of how to use this wonderful piece of poetic Zen to aid your journey. And that is just a taste of what is in the poem! There are so many other aspects I could have commented on; but I leave them for you. Please study it, and then just allow it to work on you, in your contemplative meditation.

7 Mental rehearsal
and visualisation

Why *mental* rehearsal? There are good reasons why. Firstly if you conjure up and meditate upon a scenario in your mind's eye it will lose its unfamiliarity. If you can visualise an event, then you can be better prepared for it when it occurs. Therefore fear of the unknown can be alleviated.

Champion runner Steve Cram, for example, would visualise a forthcoming race and imagine himself to be the other top competitors such as Steve Ovett or Sebastian Coe, and would then run the race as they would like it to go. He would then visualise himself replying to these tactics. So, on the day, he was mentally prepared for a variety of different scenarios.

Prior to the 1984 Olympic Games, the springboard diver Silvi Bernier undertook an intensive programme of visualising each and every dive over and over again. On the day, she kept her mind concentrated on each dive at a time. The result? Gold medal!

Robert Foster was a champion rifle shot. Because of his military duties he was unable to fire on the range for a whole year. During this time his only training was a daily session of mental rehearsal and visualisation. At the end of the year he entered a competition. The result? He broke his own World Record!

When I entered a competition I never felt stress because I was physically, psychologically and mentally prepared.

To eliminate stress from your consciousness you must be prepared to handle any contingency that may arise. You should concentrate on the task at hand *and visualise the result you want.*

(Chuck Norris)

Mike Tyson, probably the most fearsome World Heavyweight Boxing champion of the last few decades, makes use of the services of a hypnotist in the period before every fight to alleviate his fears and use the strength of his mind to build up his confidence.

Mental imagery is one of the most important areas in sport today!
(Dr. P. Mihevic, psychologist, Univ. of California)

Arnold Schwarzenegger, one of the world's greatest and best known body-builders, would always visualise the effect on his muscles of the exercises he planned, and he maintained that mental image whilst training.

In his preparation for the 400 metres event in the 1968 Olympics, Lee Evans repeatedly visualised every stride of the race. Result? Olympic Gold medal and a World Record which lasted more than ten years!

The athlete who effectively utilises his or her mental strength becomes stronger and develops greater personal control.
(T. Orlick, *Psyching for Sport*)

Joan Benoit, the woman's marathon record holder and 1984 Olympic champion, when asked to explain her success answered: 'My mental concentration, my mental toughness!'

My training wasn't to improve my physical strength or stamina; those came along as a secondary result. . .the primary purpose of every training session was *to toughen up mentally.*
(Herb Elliot, Olympic Gold Medalist and World Record holder)

Mental visualisation and rehearsal allows the practitioner to become familiar with an event *even before it actually takes place!* This provides a sense of personal control, thus alleviating the stress of entering a completely unknown environment. Visualisation of one's own technique can allow critical analysis and the opportunity to correct faults under ideal conditions.

One of the most important effects of visualisation is that one can continually rehearse applications of techniques and events, thus allowing one to achieve a level of control over them, and to build up the feeling of bringing off the techniques successfully. This leads to an increase in self-confidence, which again allows for a freer use of techniques because – once again – stress levels are kept within the beneficial arousal levels, and not allowed to have a deleterious effect.

It is a truism that any fighter who cannot visualise himself or herself under various conditions (adverse or advantageous) and has no mental plan as to what they could do in such circumstances, is more than likely to find that the circumstances will be directed by the opponent.

I must emphasise that using the method I describe it really is possible to iron out faults in technique and improve just about any aspect of physical practice.

8 *How to combine meditation with physical practice*

This chapter is really a simple step-by-step guide to mental visual-isation and rehearsal skills, practised as a form of meditation combined with physical practice as a form of biofeedback.

My own experiences may be helpful here, so I will spend some time in describing in detail how I came to invent my own form of visualisation training, and only later discovered that it was something being used quite independently by a number of top-class athletes from a variety of disciplines.

Some years ago I remember lying awake in bed at night going through in my mind the various techniques that I had been practising with *Sensei* during the regular training session, trying to get to the essence of them, and find the heart of each technique. I would lie there, continually replaying scenes from particular moments in the session when I had found that a technique had not quite worked, or, on the other hand, when a *Waza* had worked well I tried to replay the event so as to understand the lead-up to it, so that I could try it again.

After some practice, I was able to conjure up a miniature figure of myself, complete with Gi, in my imagination. I was also able to conjure up my partners and opponents where necessary, and continually replay the action over again, almost like – well, exactly like – rerunning a favourite video clip. It occurred to me that I might try to experiment with this ability and maybe utilise it in my meditation practice in a conscious attempt to correct my faults.

So, after establishing the proper degree of awareness by just following my breathing, I began to visualise a picture of myself in miniature, and it was just like watching a small T.V. screen. My *alter ego* would do the techniques exactly as I would, complete with my mistakes. I would then allow my mind to dwell on the sequence, and then begin to 'edit' it by altering the reality into a 'better' version, with the mistakes eradicated.

I would then run this sequence slowly, making sure that any changes that I had made were within the bounds of possibility. There seemed little use in getting my imaginary self do things that I would

Shiro Asano sensei – Yoko tobi geri.

Perfect concentration leading to perfect execution of technique .

The improved mawashi-geri.

An example of the end product – kisame-zuki *in action*.

find impossible in reality. Then I would gradually speed the sequence up until it was up to proper speed, and then run it over and over again, until I would be quite convinced that I really *could* do it just that way.

Actually, I was disconcerted to find that at this stage my relaxed state was a thing of the past, as my breath rate and heart rate would increase and I would almost *feel* the technique as if I were physically doing it. (I discovered later that this feeling of really doing the technique was beneficial to skill assimilation and should be encouraged.) Initially I found that I could only maintain this practice for a short while, and when my attention wandered I found it best to just relax and return to my *Zazen*.

It seemed to me that I could take the experiment further, and see if I could actually make gains in skills through allying this visualisation to actual, physical practice. At the time I was consciously trying to follow Asano sensei's advice and: 'Keep a stone face!' That is, to try and remove superfluous mannerisms, movements and expressions which would telegraph my intentions to an opponent.

So in the University Dojo I would go into a corner, kneel in *Mokuso* and begin to visualise myself in fighting stance, alert but relaxed, suddenly – with no give-away signs – shooting out a fast snap or reverse punch. I would do this for a few minutes, and then go to the large wall-mirror and take up my stance in front of it. I would stand there, and suddenly, I would have punched! No attempt to think of when to punch, but just trying to beat my own reflection! I let my body think intuitively for itself. In other words, the punch punched!

Following this, I would again kneel down in *Mokuso*, relax and imagine this time that I was facing an opponent. Keeping the same sense of intuitive striking, I would play over and over again a scenario where at the moment that I felt that my opponent was about to move I would see myself attacking so hard and fast that I would catch him dead in his tracks.

Then the final part of practice was to ask someone to partner me in one-step sparring and then free-sparring.

The end product of this experiment was that my ability to catch an opponent with a strike at the instant of his attack vastly improved, and I gained much success using this technique! From my initial experiments I found that if I set myself specific, but attainable, goals in my visualisation practice, I was definitely able to see the results.

For example, I was never – and probably never will be – satisfied with my kicking techniques. Because of a number of factors – my early Judo practice, my size (I was always the smallest fighter on the team, although I am, at 5 ft 9½ ins., of average height, but I was also stocky and not the most flexible person in the world), and the fact that I possessed very good hand speed, I found that in general I would try to close the distance between myself and an opponent as rapidly as possible in order to nullify their kicks and get into punching and sweeping range.

Anyway, I decided to see if I could improve my *mawashi-geri*, which, at the time, I was not really able to do with any real power to any target above chest height. I began to visualise myself performing the kick at *chudan* level, effortlessly and smoothly, correcting any flaws in technique which I felt might be impeding my progress and which I thought I could project into my little mind's-eye version of me.

When I found that I could make my *alter ego* kick really well at the middle-level target, I began to make the image lift the kick just a little higher, and kept running and re-running the section in my mind whilst beginning to put my spirit into it, instead of being the formerly passive observer. I began to 'feel' the technique, and convinced myself that it *was* me doing the kick, and that I *could* do it without straining, and was always able to snap back into a good strong stance.

This mental visualisation took place over a number of weeks, and I was reinforcing it by increasing my stretching and flexibility exercises.

The results were that I can now execute a far better *Jodan Mawashi-geri* with my right leg, and am still working on the left. Both kicks are now much stronger, and I now have a better choice of targets. I have also applied this method to spinning back kicks, with what I consider to be extremely good effect.

9 *The technique*

Remember that, just like the meditation practice, you must allow time for the results to show, and you must practice regularly; five to ten minutes at least five days a week is far better than twenty minutes once a week.

In fact, I find that it is useful to sit in *Mokuso* for a few minutes during regular training to use this visualisation to reinforce the physical practice. When you gain a little experience, try to imagine the feel of the technique, as you visualise it. Concentrate and really build up a deep conviction that the little figure that you can see is actually you, and that you *can* do the things that you make it do.

With this in mind, you must only set yourself realistic goals. If you know that in a million years you will never be able to perform a jumping spinning reverse-crescent kick, then there is little point in making your mind's-eye figure do it. If you set unattainable goals your visualisation will lack conviction, and when you go to try out physically what you have mentally rehearsed you will fail, and this will be counterproductive; you must establish a positive feedback. Then you will build up confidence in your practice.

So, begin by sitting quietly in your chosen meditation posture and follow your preparatory techniques for calming the mind and breathing.

Let's imagine – just for this exercise – that you want to improve your basic front kick. Start by projecting a tiny figure (don't attempt to impose any features on it at this stage) on the blank screen in your mind. Imagine this figure wearing exactly the same clothes that you would normally wear in your training, and position this figure in a well-balanced and relaxed stance.

Now start the sequence. Watch the figure do the technique just as you think you usually do, including the faults that you feel that you need to correct. See the foot snap out and back, watch the balance as the foot retracts, see the hand position throughout the kick.

Now do it again, but slow the whole thing down, and – without forcing – begin to correct the mistakes. Make the knee come up higher before snapping out the foot; check the tendency to lean back and rise up; keep the guard well up; and pull the foot back smartly so that the figure drops into a well-balanced position.

Having got the technique right in your mind, now run it through over and over again, each time a little faster, with no straining; but as you concentrate you will begin to empathise with the figure. Start to 'hear' the snap of the Gi, and the exhalation of breath. Now your heart-rate will increase and you will begin to almost feel the *Kime*. Under proper visualisation activity, the nervous system does actually send tiny signals to the muscles.

In an experiment to test this, some runners were made to lie down, and without moving imagine that they were running up a steep hill. They were then connected to an electromyograph, a device to measure muscle movement. Although no muscle movement was recorded, the machine recorded increased electrical activity in the actual muscles used in running.

Visualisation also serves to cut short the learning process, and facilitate the sending of the impulses from the brain to the muscles and back again. After all, the ultimate learning of skills, the eradication of bad habits, and so on, all takes place in the brain, and it is the brain that organises and initiates the movements of the body.

Because your martial arts training is for a lifetime, so you should be able to set different goals, over the short term and long term.

Visualisation for the competing karate-ka should concentrate upon specific areas which will reflect contest conditions and requirements.

Set the scene in your mind and become accustomed to the sights and sounds of the *Shiai-jo*.

Continually rehearse all possible situations, including making your *alter ego* face all the different types of opponents, designing game plans to deal with them. Use the practice to gain familiarity with all eventualities; thus when the event actually takes place it will not be completely foreign to you. This will alleviate a degree of the stress and tension, and make it more possible for you to take appropriate action.

Remembering that competition is only for a certain part of your martial arts life, I recommend that your visualisation practice should also concentrate upon refining the 'bread and butter' basic techniques, which will form the alphabet for every aspect of your training, regardless of your age and physical abilities.

It may seem from the above that mental visualisation and rehearsal training will take up a lot of your time. Actually, this isn't so. When you are familiar with the technique, it is better to spend not more than 10 to 15 minutes on it at any one time. It can even be usefully undertaken when it would not be possible to follow it with actual physical practice.

There is a vast amount of evidence to demonstrate that this programme can have an extremely beneficial effect, and serious karate-ka would do well to incorporate it into their regular practice.

Summary

(1) Analyse your motivation, skill-levels, strengths and weaknesses. It is necessary to know yourself realistically before attempting to make any changes.
(2) Set only realistic goals, resetting them as you achieve them.
(3) Begin a regular routine of relaxation and meditation.
(4) When proficient, extend this to include specific visualisation and rehearsal episodes.
(5) Reinforce the mental imagery with physical practice when possible. But remember that if this is not possible, mental imagery is better than nothing at all.

(6) Remember to end your physical practice whilst still strong. Exhaustion will lead to sloppy technique, and your physical reality will begin to fall short of the mental ideal; this will detract from the credibility of the mental process, so must be avoided.

10 The first attempt –
an analysis of stress

In *The Advanced Karate Manual* I gave examples of how the mind and its states strongly affect the performance of the body, and I reproduce here an extract from a report on his first karate competition by one of the FSK juniors. It is interesting as – without any prompting whatsoever – it illuminates very precisely many of the points that I made. Let's look at it first, then consider one or two of the aspects that it highlights.

'My First Competition', by Neil Sutcliffe, aged 12 (3rd Kyu)

I was terribly nervous when we arrived in Rotherham. I had entered in the under 12 year old Team Kata event, Individual and Team Kumite.

My two partners and I had chosen to perform *Hean Godan* for our Kata, and had only been practising for about two weeks prior to the competition.

My heart was beating rapidly as we marched onto the mat. 'Here goes' I thought. I looked at the referee straight in the eyes as I shouted 'Hean Godan'. One – Two – I started. My arms and legs moved like clockwork and I could see out of the corner of my eye that my partners

Kata competition with Hirokasu Kanazawa as judge.
(Kanazawa sensei awarded Vince the highest score of the
event for this Hangetsu Kata.)

were with me. 'Good!' As we came to rest in our final positions I felt confident that we hadn't made any mistakes.

The marks were given – not bad – and a cheer went up from our club supporters as we made our way off the mat. The other teams completed their Katas and we were then asked to stand to find out who was going through to the finals.

The referee shouted: 'Redhill Tigers'. That was us! I couldn't believe it, we were into the finals!

After a short break it was time for the Individual Kumite.

I felt sick as I walked over to the mat where I would be fighting. The time was ticking by as I waited and waited for my name to be called. Who was going to be my opponent? Would I remember the correct moves that I had been taught? If I didn't I would get hit!

My Dad was giving me words of encouragement as my name was called and I made my way onto the mat.

My opponent didn't look particularly mean, but I couldn't relax.

He made a dive for me and missed. I decided to wait and let him come in to me, telegraphing the move he was going to use. I side-stepped and went in and scored with a reverse punch. I thought about being adventurous and using a front kick, but decided against it as I might leave myself open for a hit!

Again he came in, and again I scored. This wasn't so bad after all!

I scored yet again, and suddenly it was over and I had won my first round – first ever – fight!

As I waited for my next opponent fear started to slowly creep back into me and I felt jittery as I listened to instructions and encouragement.

Then I was back on the mat.

This opponent started off very lively, throwing punches and kicks everywhere, but missing. His *Sensei* told him to slow down, and so he just stood there waiting for me to make a move.

I started moving from side to side feigning punches. I thought about going in a few times but uncertainty stopped me, and I waited a bit longer.

I heard the 30 seconds bell. We both stood there looking at each other.

One of us had to make a move. Suddenly I leapt in with a reverse punch which fortunately landed right on target, giving me a ½ point, and winning the match.

I walked off the mat and immediately burst into tears. Fear, excitement, disbelief all rushing around in my head. My heart was pounding and I felt sick. I didn't want to go on – I had to go on. I was through to the Quarter-finals and didn't want to let anybody down!

(Neil's nerves finally got the better of him in his next fight, when he fought an opponent from a different style, whose coach helped to intimidate Neil by shouting remarks like: 'Get him! Get him, he's easy!')

Round three, onto the mat again, opponent's style was Kung Fu. He was wearing a black suit. He looked mean and angry. I could see the letters 'Kill!' written on his eyeballs! My legs turned to jelly. I didn't want to fight him but I had to, had to! Here we go, let's get it over with!

He came straight for me and scored. His *Sensei* was on the sidelines shouting: 'Beautiful. Go in again, he's easy!'

I felt like socking him in the face (as) he kept on shouting: 'Get him. Get him!'

I was wishing (that) the ground would open up and swallow me up. No control. I had to gain control.

In he came again with a kick and scored. I tried to get myself to move forward and go for him, but he came in with a punch and scored for the third time. It was all over. I had lost the round. I walked off the mat choked, disappointed and drained. My parents were patting me on the back and telling me that I done well, but I was frustrated and angry with myself for not trying harder.

At the end of the tournament Neil went home with a Kata trophy and a lot of experience to build on for the future.

If we look at Neil's report in greater detail we can see some of the classic examples of malfunction under pressure or stress.

Some of the stress is external in origin (the unfamiliar appearance of the opponent, the opponent's apparent confidence, the disturbing shouts from the opponent's coach undermining Neil's self-confidence etc.,) whilst other stresses are internally produced ('I didn't want to go on . . . I had to go on . . . *I didn't want to let anyone down!'*)

The former is fear of the unknown, and gives credence to the ancient martial arts adage: In any situation if you know neither your enemy nor yourself, then the likely outcome is failure. If you know your adversary but not yourself, then the odds are evenly balanced. When you know your opponent *and* yourself, you cannot be beaten.

Neil was afraid because he was in a strange environment – the competition – his opponent was not wearing the same colour Gi that he was familiar with, his style was also different, and he was subjected to further pressure by the shouts of his opponent's coach. He was also under stress because he did not feel that his own skill was sufficient to deal with the situation. He did not have sufficient self-confidence.

His situation was made worse because he further added to his own anxiety by loading himself with 'future guilt': he was not able to be detached and concentrate only on the encounter, because he also carried 'responsibility' towards his coach, club and his parents. He did not want to 'let them down'!

Now all types of stress lead to tension. In the right degree this is beneficial, as it leads to a state of positive arousal which enables the body to function at peak efficiency. Too much, however, impairs the body's efficiency and psychologically leads to feelings of panic, confusion, a feeling of fatigue, depression, a sense of nausea, lack of co-ordination and the inability to work to the levels demanded by the brain; thus more stress is fed into the equation.

The result for Neil was that his legs 'turned to jelly', and he showed the typical stressed resolve: 'Let's get it over with!'

What is the answer, then? Well, the first thing to accept is that if Neil (or anyone else, for that matter) simply continues to practise in the same way, then except for perhaps gaining some familiarity with the ambience of competition merely through continuing to take part, they will never become free of their extraneous baggage of self-imposed stress.

The Samurai were encouraged to begin each day by imagining the many ways in which it could be their last. They would consider their end. Be it by sword, arrow or even by their own hand. Of course, this would seem a little inappropriate for just a competition, but the underlying concept remains valid. Spending some time in contemplation of the worst that might happen has a twofold effect.

Firstly it accustoms one to facing up to failure; but more importantly it begins to make one aware of how silly most of one's fears actually are. It also allows the opportunity of devising tactics to help deal with the problem and perhaps prevent the worst from happening. Note that Neil's report never stressed his fears for himself, nor any possible injury that he might suffer. I am sure that he did have these fears, but the ones that he thought it important to mention were fears of how his friends and family might react if he 'let them down'.

Just as the Samurai considered the results of their failure, so should the modern martial artist, whether in competition or not. Would Neil have had to leave home because his parents would not love him if he did not win his match? Would he be ostracised by his friends, maybe asked to leave his Dojo? As parents, would our children despise us if we just couldn't afford that foreign holiday? Do we really imagine that our businesses would collapse into bankruptcy should we ever be ill, or simply take time off to be with our families? And so on.

Ridiculous isn't it? Yet in many aspects of life we are all guilty of putting ourselves under wholly unrealistic pressure.

All training *must* pay attention to the power of the mind. Meditation, plus mental rehearsal and visualisation should form part of every martial artist's way of life. In this manner the spirit can remain strong and fearless, in the face of all odds, even when our physical strength starts to decline.

Even the old masters accepted that an unsophisticated fighter with tremendous spirit could give a good account of himself against a more skilful but less mentally committed opponent. Calm, concentrated awareness, *Zanshin*, does not come about without training, and the mind must undergo it in the same way as the body. Then this inner strength can be utilised in all of life's encounters, not just in the *Shiai-jo*.

11 A final note

When I was much younger, and a singer in a rock and roll band, for good or ill I had the facility to sing very much like Elvis Presley. It wasn't forced, except for the American accent, but then, you try singing proper rock and roll in a typical English accent! It doesn't work.

Anyway, it led to a certain amount of acclaim, which at first I found flattering, especially when American audiences also found it remarkable. The trouble was that, in the end, people were only asking me to sing Elvis songs; they were not really interested in me sounding like me! There was a time when agents wanted me to dress up in a white rhinestone-bedecked suit and travel around performing shows as an Elvis impersonator. I thought about it, but in the end I refused, and even though I still sang Elvis numbers I always changed them in some way; either the arrangement, or the rhythm, – and I never wore the suit!

The point is, that you must never try to be *like* Buddha, or Christ, or like any other teacher or leader. You must follow what is wise in their teachings, but never wear their clothes! Find the essence of your own life; tear down illusion and become the finest, most magnificent You!

At the end of it all, remember that to spend the whole of your life and energy in the attempt to become the most dangerous and successful fighter of all, would not only be useless, but a sad and shameful waste. There is more, much more to life than becoming a pseudo-Samurai.

History reveals time and again, by the barbaric nature of the acts carried out in wartime by the supposed epitomes of Bushido, that the ethic was seldom borne out in practice.

I will remind you of Asano sensei's advice regarding the purpose of karate training: 'If you just want to win fights, then go and buy a shotgun!'

Your training and meditation away from the Dojo should enhance your efforts in the Dojo: your efforts in the Dojo should enhance everything that you do!

If you want to, you can write to me c/o the FSK.

Charles Mack, Vince's first Karate sensei.

Vince aged eighteen.

Vince receiving the SKI British Team Championship trophy
from Asano sensei.

On the TV set of 'Chancer', with Derek Fowlds and Philip Stone.

*Still playing that rock and roll! Vince at home on piano,
and in performance with backing singers.*

About the Author

The author, currently a 5th Dan, FSK Team Coach and former successful British and European Squad member in Kumite and Kata, has long been a student of Zen Buddhism and various types of meditation and its conjunction with martial arts training.

Vince began his training at the age of fourteen, when he started to practise Judo. He was naturally suited to this art, and soon progressed from club medalist to participating successfully at national level.

At the age of fifteen, Vince left home and grammar school to become a musician and singer in a number of rock bands, and this was his main career for the next ten years or so. During this time he maintained his Judo practice, until he heard of the 'new' art of Karate.

He began his training in London under the powerful figure of Charles Mack, an outstanding Judo player who had spent years training in Japan. Whilst there, Charlie had also gained black-belt status in Aikido and Karate, at the JKA.

Following his desire to continue the education that he had left so early, Vince left London and was accepted as a mature student into the English Department at Nottingham University, and it was at this time that he became a student of Shiro Asano 8th Dan, who had been recommended to the Nottingham Karate group as a resident instructor by Hirokasu Kanazawa.

Vince trained regularly at Asano sensei's Dojo for the next twelve years, becoming one of his senior students, and a regular member of the Shotokan Karate International Open British Championship winning team for many years. He was also a member of the successful International Squad in both Kumite and Kata.

During this period Vince was also selected and fought successfully for the British Universities International Karate Team. He also captained the Nottingham University team to win the British Championships, and was awarded a University Gold for consistent excellence and achievement at National and International level.

On the political scene, Vince established the English Karate Federation, which went on to become the governing body for English Karate. He was elected first Vice-Chairman, then Chairman of the Martial Arts Commission, the governing body for all martial arts; a position he resigned when he was unable to bring about agreement for Karate to stand alone, to regulate and rule itself, in the same manner as the British Judo Association. Vince is also a qualified referee.

The successful SKI European squad, author far right.

As an author, Vince has written and co-written with his friend and colleague, former World Champion Aidan Trimble, some eight best-selling books on the martial arts, which are sold throughout the world, even in Japan. They are currently working on a screen-play and a novel dealing with international terrorism.

Following on his musical career by becoming a successful business-man with special interests in Fine Art, Vince is also making a name for himself (but what he won't say!) in the acting profession, with appearances in many T.V. series such as 'Chancer', 'Boon', 'Hard Cases' and others.

Vince has a reputation as a strong-spirited karate-ka, who insists upon the pragmatic reality of training. His test is 'Does it work?'

None the less, whilst continually emphasising the importance of competition only as an adjunct to traditional training, Vince has used his considerable experience with success. His students are consistent medal winners in the Federation of Shotokan Karate championships;

Coaching the FSK squad, Las Vegas 1990.

in 1990 winning both 1st and 2nd places in the Team Kumite, 1st and 3rd place in the Men's Individual Kumite, 1st Place in the Junior Kumite, 1st place in the Women's Individual Kumite and 2nd in the Women's Kata event, as well as also regularly winning medals at National Open events. He was coach to the British team at the 1990 JKA World Championships in Dubhai.

As the Asst. Chief Instructor to the FSK, Vince teaches throughout Britain and Europe. He also shares the coaching responsibilities with the Chief Instructor, Aidan Trimble.

Notes to the text

1 Master Higaonna would not have anyone of bad character as a student, and would expel any student who failed to live up to expectations.

2 In martial arts terms, is the runner-up to the World Champion a failure?

   If you fill a pint pot to the brim, is a half-pint pot a failure because when full it only holds half as much? Of all the students in your class, which is the failure? They are all trying 100% to improve. Some progress more quickly; are the rest failures? Have you given up yet? No: then when have you failed? You might not win every fight: neither did Mike Tyson; will you call him a failure? See?

3 Medical science attests to the undeniable powers of the mind to bring about both psychological and physiological changes. Hypnotism, for example, is now a recognised medical tool used to effect changes in motivation, self-confidence, the breaking of harmful habits, and so on.

   The placebo effect, where pseudo-medicines have been found to bring about physical benefits when administered instead of the actual medicine, is such an established concept that drug trials actually incorporate it into their research techniques.

   On a wider scale, there is a great deal of evidence that visualisation techniques during meditation have directly brought about improvements in medical conditions. The American actress Shirley Maclaine tells of her experiences in this area, to name just one well-known example; and the powers of the mind are also being channelled by many into fighting the ravages of cancer.

To look even further afield, note the formidable powers of the Witch Doctor, and Ju-Ju man.

4 Zen had previously enjoyed a brief popularity in Japan in the seventh century, but did not really establish itself until the reintroduction by Eisai in 1191/2. It was Eisai, by the way, who also introduced tea into Japan, where it was first admired for its medicinal qualities, and later – curiously enough – acquired further Zen connections when becoming the centre-piece of another meditational type of practice, the Tea Ceremony, which was even carried out as a method of calming the mind and refocussing the spirit prior to (and in some cases, during) actual battles.

5 See also the remarks of Zen master, calligrapher and artist, Hakuin (1685–1768): 'Sometimes you may feel that you are getting nowhere with your practice of meditation in the rush of life. On the other hand, when you sit quietly you get some results. But, be sure that those who sit quietly can never hope to enter into meditation in activity.

'Meditation in the midst of activity is immeasurably superior to simply sitting quietly. If you do not become able to meditate even within your worldly duties your progress is almost impossible!'

6 *The Karate-do Manual*, by P.M.V. Morris (Stanley Paul, 1979).

7 One of the most succinct expositions of *Zanshin* was made by the Zen master Takuan (1573–1645) to his most famous pupil, the legendary swordsman Yagyu-Tajima-no-kami, who was himself teacher of swordsmanship to the shogun:

> "Where should the mind be placed in a duel with swords? If it is set on the opponent's movements, it stops there. If it is set on his sword, it stops there. If on the thought of killing him, it stops with that thought. If on one's own sword, it stops there. If on the thought of not being killed by him, it stops with that thought. Where should it be set if one wants it to function freely, without check?

Some people say, then isn't it better to keep the mind on the *Tanden* just below the navel? This is good, but it is not the highest attainment . . . in fact, if it is set anywhere, you will be restricted. The answer is to have no idea at all about setting the mind. If you can avoid setting it in any particular place, it will pervade the entire body, down to the tips of the fingers and toes.

[Then] If hands are to move, they obey the mind at once; if the eyes are to look about, they instantly follow the order of the mind. Therefore mind is not to be focussed on any part of the body."

8 One of the qualities which was expected of a good student of Zen was that even in the direst crisis he would remain calm and controlled.

When the *Soto* monk Sogyo was set upon and held upside-down off a high bridge over a river by thugs, they demanded to know what he had got to say:

> Snow and ice on the mountain peak,
> The rushing torrent in the valley.

Not only was he not afraid, but he was even able to present his fearless reply in verse! They let him go.

Recommended books and works consulted

Bushido, the Way of the Warrior, John Newman. Magna Books, 1989.

The Samurai: a Military History, S.R. Turnbull. Osprey, 1977.

Sport Psychology, W.F. Straub. Movement Publications, 1978.

Sporting Excellence, D. Hemery. Wm. Collins, 1986.

The Zen Way to the Martial Arts, T. Deshimaru. Century, 1982.

The TM Technique, P. Russell. RKP, 1976.

The Winning Mind, P. Terry. Thorsons, 1989.

Maximum Sports Performance, J.F. Fixx. Angus, 1986.

The Warrior Koans, T. Leggett. Arkania, 1985.

The Book of the Samurai, S.R. Turnbull. Magna, 1982.

Bushido, J. Newman. Magna, 1989.

Zen Training, K. Sekida. Weatherhill, 1975.

The Awakened Mind, C. M. Cade. Wildwood House, 1979.

Karate-do Nyumon, Gichin Funakoshi. Kodansha, 2nd edn., 1988.

Okinawan Karate, M. Bishop. Black, 1989.

Address for correspondence

The Federation of Shotokan Karate
PO Box 47
West PDO
Nottingham NG8 2EA
England